Echoes of Forgotten Memories

In a dusty chest, old tunes twine,
A sock with holes, once a shoe divine.
A rubber chicken sings with glee,
As I laugh at nostalgia's spree.

Lost marbles swirl in a playful dance,
A yo-yo spins, lost in a trance.
Forgotten jokes, all told in jest,
Bring back the days when we were blessed.

Original title:
The Trunk Tales

Copyright © 2025 Creative Arts Management OÜ
All rights reserved.

Author: Hugo Fitzgerald
ISBN HARDBACK: 978-1-80567-230-2
ISBN PAPERBACK: 978-1-80567-529-7

Journeys in a Weathered Box

Once I found a map, oh what a thrill,
Leading to candy on top of the hill.
But curiously it led me back home,
Where my cat claimed the prize, with a sassy comb.

A compass that spins, drives me to grin,
Each wild adventure is a splendid win.
With every trip, laughter grows wide,
In this box, every secret resides.

Treasures of Time Unraveled

An old clock ticks, but what a tease,
Always running late, it never agrees.
With every chime, a story unfolds,
Of mishaps and giggles, oh what it holds.

A mirror reflects a clownish grin,
Reminding me of the goofy within.
With trinkets stacked that wobble and gleam,
The laughter of years is the best of dreams.

Shadows in the Wooden Crate

In a crate where shadows play,
A jester's cap has lost its sway.
With giggly whispers and a wink so sly,
The past comes alive, oh me, oh my!

Old toys peek out, ready to tease,
In a world where giggles flutter like leaves.
With each hidden gem, a chuckle is found,
In the shadows, joy knows no bound.

Remnants of Time Encased

Once there was a chest so stout,
Inside it hid a strange old sprout.
With socks that danced and shoes that sang,
A funny smell, as chaos sprang.

Old maps of places never found,
With treasures wrapped yet tightly bound.
A rubber chicken, laughter's friend,
These oddities that never end.

A pair of glasses, cracked and round,
Said, 'Let's explore the world around!'
With every item, a giggle burst,
Each story shared, till laughter cursed.

So pop the lid and take a peek,
In dusty treasures, joy we seek.
From silly things, hilarity blooms,
In this wild chest, life always zooms.

Hidden Journeys in Faded Leather

A suitcase worn from travel tales,
With mice that dance and fish that wails.
Buttons missing like tiny stars,
As whispers echo from afar.

Inside this bag, a world unfolds,
With tales of mischief, joy retold.
Adventures gone and laughter spry,
A hat that claimed it made you fly.

Pajamas worn on trips to space,
And spoons that danced in a warm embrace.
Oh, what a ride, this quirky flight,
With everything wrong feeling just right!

So unzip the past and take it in,
Each hidden journey, a joyful spin.
In faded leather, stories thrive,
Where humor lives and spirits dive.

The Keeper of Old Whispers

In a dusty attic, secrets smirk,
A whimsical crow begins to lurk.
With tales of socks that went to parties,
And spoons that joined in on the jollies.

Old letters penned in scribbled guise,
With laughter trapped in ink that lies.
Whispers float, they tickle the ear,
Of days gone by, filled with cheer.

A fur coat purring with feline glee,
Plays hide and seek with a history.
Each oddity brings a chuckle loud,
Amongst the whispers, jokes abound.

So listen closely to stories spun,
In laughter's lap, we've just begun.
For in this space where echoes play,
The keeper's tales will bright our day.

Beneath the Canopy of Secrets

There's a squirrel with tales so grand,
He digs them up, just like a band.
He whispers secrets in the breeze,
As branches giggle, swaying with ease.

The owls hoot truths by moonlit light,
While frogs croak jokes, a comical sight.
Leaves chatter softly, sharing delight,
Nature's humor, a wondrous night.

Ephemeral Echoes in Timber

In hollow logs, mischief is stored,
Where beetles plot, and fun is poured.
A raccoon spills tales over berries,
While ants burst in laughs, so light and merry.

Echoes of giggles dance in the wood,
As whispers fly, oh, isn't it good?
Nature's folly, a grand masquerade,
With every twist, a prank is played.

Unraveling Stories from Within

Behind the bark, there's laughter brewing,
A family of rabbits, always skewing.
They weave their yarns with tiny paws,
Creating chaos, without a pause.

A hedgehog scribbles in leafy scrolls,
He pens the antics of silly souls.
With giggles echoing through the night,
Woodland humor, a pure delight.

The Weight of Time Encased

Old branches creak with stories old,
Of mushrooms who danced under rain so bold.
Their fungus parties, a riotous bash,
With sprinkles of laughter, an epic splash.

As time ticks by, with a chuckle and wink,
The forest unfolds all it can think.
Through seasons of jest and whimsical play,
Each gnarled knot holds joy in its sway.

The Vessel of Forgotten Dreams

In a corner, hidden away,
Lies a chest where socks go to play.
Old shoes whisper secrets of dance,
While a shirt dreams of one last chance.

A map to nowhere, some crumbs of toast,
The ghost of a sandwich, no one will boast.
A rusted key, a notebook too,
What treasures await? If only they knew!

Legacies Lying in Wait

Under the stairs, a box full of spice,
A sock puppet army, it looks so nice!
Grandpa's old glasses, a rubber band ball,
A broken old clock that doesn't tick at all.

Each item a story, a jester's delight,
Spinning tall tales of improbable flight.
A spoon that once stirred a pot of joy,
Now plays hide and seek with an old toy.

Where History Awaits

There's a hat that once graced a cat in a play,
And a whip made from yarn for a horse made of clay.
With tales of old pirates who fought on the sea,
And a rubber duck squawking, "Come sail home with me!"

Maps of lost civilizations made of cheese,
And a knight on a mission, just hoping to please.
It's history's laughter, a raucous display,
Where every odd item wants to have its say!

Echoing Silences of Lost Adventures

What stories lie dormant, just waiting for cheer?
A relic of laughter, a half-eaten pair.
A kite that once soared, now tangled in dreams,
When the wind was a friend with powerful beams.

Old tickets to shows that nobody saw,
Teacups that witness a majestic haul.
In this treasure of banter, with giggles we find,
Adventures unspoken, they're all intertwined.

Relics of the Overgrown Path

In a forest thick and lush,
Old shoes sprout like mushrooms,
A hat sits high on a green bush,
Wondering why it's lost its homes.

Beneath a log, a treasure lies,
A sandwich long forgotten,
With ants making their tiny spies,
Claiming it, now it's been rotten.

A bike rusts where kids once sped,
But squirrels found it fun to ride,
They giggle and to the world they fled,
While humans shake their heads and sighed.

So stroll along with smiles wide,
For nature holds a quirky charm,
In every corner, secrets hide,
To tickle your heart without harm.

Ancient Roots

Deep down where the wildflowers wave,
A gnome sits with a grin so sly,
Poking fun at the foolish brave,
Who walk by and never ask why.

A raccoon dons a crown of leaves,
Thinks he's king of this leafy land,
Follows wherever mischief weaves,
With a tail that's perfectly planned.

Beneath the branches, laughter swells,
As critters swap their playful tales,
The wise old owl casts friendly spells,
While the rabbits measure their trails.

So cherish that laughter, bright and true,
For nature's jesters chew life's threads,
And if you listen, it's all for you,
These ancient roots dance 'neath your heads.

Hidden Dreams

In the crook of an ancient tree,
A fox dreams of a grand parade,
With toadstools prancing, wild and free,
Beneath the stars, a cool cascade.

Mice build castles made of cheese,
While owls host the evening show,
The forest chuckles in the breeze,
As moonlight turns the fields aglow.

Each shadow tells a silly joke,
With fireflies lighting up the night,
The wind carries tales as it stokes,
Our giggles swim in pure delight.

So wander where the wild things play,
And let your heart explore its schemes,
For in the woods, come what may,
You'll find the magic of those dreams.

Treasures of the Timeless Tree

Beneath branches wide and proud,
Nuts and acorns stage a show,
While squirrels chatter in a crowd,
Debating how to steal the glow.

A chipmunk's wearing a bright sock,
Claims it's fashion, what a sight!
While bees buzz to a ticking clock,
Hurrying to end their flight.

Old roots hide stories, just for you,
Like whispers of a world unseen,
In laughter, every tale rings true,
Nature's pranksters keep it keen.

So gather 'round this leafy stage,
Where secrets twinkle in the leaves,
Each moment sparks a joyful page,
In life's book, laughter never leaves.

Beneath Layers of Life

Underneath a carpet of green,
Lies history buried, rough and gruff,
With worms who tell tales often seen,
That even gold can't make up for tough.

A toppled log here makes a throne,
For creatures armed with charm so bright,
With beetles spinning tales of 'stone',
And frogs croaking rhymes at night.

The air is thick with giggling sounds,
As nature's jesters take the stage,
With laughter echoing all around,
In a wondrous, slightly silly age.

So take a step, get down and see,
The roots, the wiggles, all in line,
For in this chaos, you'll find the key,
To laughter that will always shine.

The Forgotten Keeper of Tales

In a dusty room where shadows play,
A keeper of secrets mislaid, they say.
With spectacles perched on his nose so wide,
He chuckles at gossip the dust cannot hide.

Old maps and trinkets clutter his floor,
Each telling a story, and maybe more.
He spins tall tales with a wink and a grin,
Of pirates, lost treasures, and where you've been.

A parrot named Jasper squawks, 'What's the scoop?'
As they plot to unravel the wildest loop.
With each quirky artifact under his care,
He brings laughter and wonders for all who dare.

So if you find him in a cozy nook,
Just pull up a chair, take a good look.
You'll hear all the laughter, glories, and flails,
From the keeper of stories, the master of tales.

Threads of Eternity

In a world of yarns and colors bright,
Spools of laughter twist and take flight.
Grandma's old sewing kit always spills,
With tales of mischief and sewing thrills.

A needle's sharp, but the stories are sharper,
Of stitches that played the role of a parter.
Fabric and laughter woven in seams,
Each stitch carries tales of odd dreams.

In corners where sock monsters come to play,
And a button's lost, yet it finds its way.
Quilts draped with whimsy and a patch or two,
Hold memories of mishaps from years gone through.

So come, grab a thread, let's spin and weave,
In this quirky world, who would believe?
Every loop tells a joke, every knot a laugh,
In the threads of eternity, we share our path.

Secrets Enshrined in Wooden Walls

In the creaky corners of an old wooden house,
Lies a collection of secrets, as quiet as a mouse.
The walls whisper softly to those who will hear,
Of sock thieves and laughter from yesteryear.

A nail pops out, an old photo falls,
Revealing great-grandpa making funny calls.
With a laugh and a jig, he danced on the floor,
Chasing grandma who ran out the door.

A closet hides stories of dressing up odd,
Strange hats and capes, and mischief they trod.
While shadows recount the tales of delight,
Of wild birthday parties that lasted all night.

So listen closely as the wood beams creak,
They share secrets of fun, and this is no peek!
In the heart of the house, where memories dwell,
Funny tales linger, ah, the stories they tell.

Tucked Away Wonders

Beneath the stairs, in a chest stuffed tight,
Lies a trove of wonders that beckon with light.
Old toys and trinkets, odd socks and hats,
Celebrating the days when life was all spats.

A spinning top wobbles, a yo-yo swings high,
Each item tucked away has a reason why.
Giggling dolls wink from corners so sly,
They've weathered the years with a mischievous eye.

Neon flashbacks of jokes that fell flat,
From rubber chickens to a squeaky old cat.
Each nook is alive with giggles and glee,
Inviting the bravest to come take a peek.

So dig through the wonders, don't leave them alone,
Each tucked-away treasure can lighten your tone.
Embrace the oddities, let laughter unfold,
In this chest of wonders, pure joy to behold.

The Forgotten Atlas

In a dusty grove, I found a map,
Dotting places on a scribbled scrap.
Turning it upside down in pure delight,
My cat now rules the land, day and night.

Each X a secret, or maybe a pie,
But it led me nowhere, oh my, oh my!
A treasure hunt in my backyard,
For buried snacks, that's not too hard!

Treasures Folded in Silence

In a treasure chest locked tight with age,
I found my socks, the mystery's stage.
Where's the gold? Nowhere to be found,
Just odd memories wrapped all around.

Old birthday cards with doodles so wild,
And letters from friends, bursting with styled.
Silent treasures, full of surprise,
More fun than gold, these memories rise!

Memories that Time Forgot

Dusty old albums, forgotten and neat,
Worn faces smiling, oh what a treat!
Mustaches so funny, and hair so grand,
Did everyone pose with a rubber band?

Granny's pink slippers in all of their glory,
Every snapshot tells a goofy story.
Time played tricks, but laughter stays,
In these funny flashbacks, time always plays!

Fragments of a Wanderer's History

Stamps in my passport, prices too high,
Unique souvenirs, like a potato pie.
Maps that crisscross like spaghetti on fire,
Every trip's spice, oh who needs a flyer?

From mountains to beaches, missteps galore,
Lost in translation, but who keeps score?
All of these tales with a wiggle and jig,
Life's a dance, just tap it, my friend, give a big gig!

Whispers of Worn Fabric

In a closet so tight, where the old things reside,
A sock with a hole, and a sweater with pride.
They gossip and chuckle in a playful old way,
As memories flutter, they dance and they sway.

The hats tip their brims with a silly, sly grin,
Old coats tell stories of adventures within.
The trousers conspire, they stretch and they fold,
In a world made of cotton, they're silly and bold.

Reclaiming the Hidden Heritage

Underneath dust, lives a quilt with a tale,
Of grandma's wild parties and flours from hail.
Each patch holds a giggle, each seam has a joke,
Beneath all the layers, there's laughter bespoke.

That old trunk holds treasures, a mix-matched crew,
Of spoons, and odd toys that still wish they flew.
A badge from a race with a story so grand,
In the attic they plot how to start a rock band.

Forgotten Paths in a Wooden Box

In a chest made of oak, lies a world gone awry,
A rubber duck army just waiting to fly.
They plan their next mission, with giggles and glee,
"Let's conquer the bathtub," they shout with esprit!

Beneath all the clutter, there's a maze built with flair,
Where marbles roll swiftly like they haven't a care.
Old maps chart adventures to undefined lands,
Where mischief awaits with pancake-making hands.

Tucked Away Dreams and Wishes

In a drawer so deep, where the dreams like to hide,
A paper airplane and a cat with some pride.
They scheme for the day they take flight with a chirp,
While that old yo-yo twirls with a playful little burp.

A glittery wish bone, a secret to share,
Hopes crammed in a corner, dust bunnies aware.
With a wink and a nudge, they conspire and plot,
For a world made of giggles, they'll give it a shot.

Recollections of a Wanderer's Pack

Once I found a sock so grand,
It danced on my feet, not as I planned.
A map of crumbs I thought was neat,
But led me straight to a dog named Pete.

In pockets deep, I found a toy,
A squeaky thing, it brought me joy.
It rumbled loud, it rolled away,
And gave the cat a fright today.

Memories Wrapped in Burlap

Beneath the wrap of faded cloth,
A treasure trove? A dusty moth!
Old receipts from places long gone,
And a rubber chicken still has its dawn.

A sandwich left from '94,
It brought the ants, oh what a score!
With laughter ringing in the air,
The memories hang, a comical flair.

Notes from an Abandoned Attic

In the attic, strange notes reside,
One stuck to an old, ragged ride.
It told of a ghost with a jolly grin,
Who danced with socks, wearing blue skin.

A rubber band ball with tales to tell,
Of epic battles and a life so swell.
But alas, it's just a duct-tape fight,
With laughter echoing well into the night.

Beneath the Surface of Dust

Underneath the dust and gloom,
A treasure map led to a broom.
But what I found was such delight,
An old hat that made my head look trite.

With shoes that squeaked and jumped so high,
I chased a broomstick 'neath the sky.
It led me to a game of chase,
With all my friends in silly space.

Whispers of Forgotten Wood

In a forest where giggles bloom,
Trees tell jokes with a creaking boom.
A squirrel chortles, a raccoon grins,
Sharing secrets of where the fun begins.

Leaves dance lightly, rustling their chat,
A wise old owl wearing a silly hat.
The mushrooms chuckle, wearing spots so bright,
As shadows play tag in the fading light.

Secrets Beneath the Bark

Beneath the bark, whispers take flight,
A beetle plays cards with a worm at night.
They bet on rain or the coming sun,
In a world where the laughter is never done.

A woodpecker pecks out a beat so sweet,
While ants line up for a dance on their feet.
Every crevice holds a raucous tale,
Of daring escapes and a snail's grand sail.

Stories Carved in Time

On wooden walls, tales start to glow,
A raccoon flips pages, putting on a show.
There's a saga of rings, each one a laugh,
Of how the old tree avoided the saw's path.

Ancient carvings, a wizard's prank,
A troll with braces, he's changing his rank.
Frog choruses sing, with croaks like a tune,
Celebrating events 'neath a big, round moon.

Echoes from the Old Chest

In a chest once dusty and snug,
Lies a mischievous monkey wearing a mug.
He tells of treasures not found in gold,
But of laughter shared and adventures bold.

Maps with scribbles and riddles collide,
A treasure hunt where the giggles bide.
With every old echo, a story unfurls,
Of playful pranks in a world of squirrels.

Yarn of Yesterday

In a box so wide, treasures align,
Old socks, a spoon, a lost shoelace twine.
Each item whispers secrets with glee,
Like a squirrel in a hat, so wild and free.

A beat-up toy car, a rubbery frog,
Pigeon feathers and a half-eaten log.
Grandpa's old glasses, one lens now cracked,
Catching laughter in all the things stacked.

A tattered glove with no mate in sight,
It waves goodnight in the soft moonlight.
With every discovery, giggles abound,
Nostalgic treasures, hilariously found.

The memories roll, like a silly song,
In this quirky trove where we all belong.
So gather round, let's take a look,
At the funny tales from this treasure book.

The Memories of an Unclosed Book

Pages flutter like birds on the run,
With ink-splattered words, oh what fun!
A splash of juice stains, a doodle or two,
A mishap caught whilst trying to chew.

The hero is a cat wearing silly hats,
Chasing after feathery, plump little rats.
Each adventure spills giggles and cheer,
With rhymes that tickle and stories so queer.

A bookmark that's folded, an envelope torn,
As if the book's saying, 'I wasn't worn!'
From love notes to doodles, a patchwork of life,
Unfolding tales, with laughter in strife.

Flip through the pages, close your eyes tight,
Hear each little chuckle in the moonlight.
This book's still unsealed, with stories untold,
From the jests of the past to the joys of the old.

Tails of Untold Journeys

Wagging behind, the tales they spin,
Of a fish that outswam a curious grin.
A rabbit in boots, hopping on the track,
Chasing his hat that flew with a quack.

Through puddles and mud, they dance with delight,
Each tail a story, oh what a sight!
There's a cat in a cape, flying so high,
With dreams made of clouds, brushed by the sky.

Off to the moon, a haphazard flight,
With cookies and giggles, it's pure delight.
Swapping silly tales with a wise old stump,
Laughter erupting with each little thump.

So gather your tails and spin them with flair,
For each furry friend has a tale to share.
Adventures await with each wagging toe,
In a world of nonsense where anything goes.

Mementos of the Roads Not Taken

A shoe with a sole that's oddly misplaced,
Leads to a journey none could have faced.
With mismatched laces, it struts and sways,
Charting new paths through a whimsical maze.

A map marked with X's that led nowhere fast,
Filled with hot chocolate spills from travels past.
Each street sign a giggle, a detour or two,
Spicing up stories that no one once knew.

Confetti from parties that never took place,
Crammed in the pockets of an old winter space.
Every moment a spark, a laugh in disguise,
Turning the ordinary into a prize.

So cherish those moments, both silly and bright,
For in laughter we find what makes life light.
Adventures missed yet humorously found,
In the roads not taken, joy knows no bounds.

Fables from the Storage Room

In a box of mismatched socks,
A stowaway squirrel laughs and talks.
He tells of treasure, old and grand,
While rummaging through a rubber band.

A dusty hat that once was cool,
Holds secrets of a long-lost school.
The buttons dance, the ribbons sway,
As they plan their great escape today.

A sandwich in a tupperware,
Whispers tales of an ancient pair.
They say it's stale, it says it's fine,
"I'll take a bite," says a cat named Whine.

In jars of marbles, stories dwell,
Of epic games we know too well.
Each one's a hero, bold and bright,
Who fought for victory, day and night.

Unearthing the Past

Beneath the floorboards, what a find,
A rubber chicken, one of a kind.
It squawks tales of the fun it had,
With a circus troupe, oh, how it's rad!

A dusty globe spins tales of yore,
It points to places nevermore.
'Round the world in a curious hour,
With maps of pudding and candy flour.

Old photographs with silly grins,
Reveal the mischief, and where it begins.
Beware the mustache — it has a grin,
That makes you wonder what lies within.

From every corner, laughter springs,
Of wacky hats and silly things.
Unearthed treasures, what a blast,
Each one holding a giggle from the past.

Tales of Tattered Keepsakes

In a suitcase, once bright and bold,
Lay secrets of adventures untold.
A tie that sings and a shoe that twirls,
Each keepsake giggles, each memory unfurls.

A deck of cards with faces strange,
Holds whispers of love, and a little change.
They shuffle and deal with winks and grins,
Creating magic that never thins.

An old toy robot with rusty knees,
Tells stories that float upon the breeze.
He beeps and boops, a comical show,
With moves so stiff, it steals the glow.

A forgotten diary with riddles trapped,
Holds laughter from those who napped.
Unlock the joy in faded lines,
And discover the mirth that always shines.

Hidden in the Chest

In a treasure chest beneath the bed,
Lies a jester's hat and a loaf of bread.
The bread says "Eat!" while the hat just jives,
A comedy duo that endlessly thrives.

A lonely rubber duck demands a stage,
To quack and quip like a crafty sage.
With bath-time antics that make us laugh,
He splashes around on a bubble bath staff.

Amidst the toys and forgotten letters,
Reside the giggles of silly betters.
Each crumb of laughter, each doodle drawn,
Creates a tale from dusk until dawn.

Secrets of joy, all hidden away,
In the chest where memories play.
Open the lid and let them out,
For fun and laughter are what it's about!

Lost Letters in a Dusty Attic

In an attic so high, with dust all around,
Letters whisper secrets, their voices profound.
One says, 'Dear friend, I stole your last pie!'
While another recounts how a cat learned to fly.

Beneath cobwebs and shadows, the papers conspire,
Of crushes and mishaps that never expire.
Each fold holds a giggle, each ink blot a tear,
A treasure of laughter, all stored in good cheer.

In this attic of wonders, the stories collide,
Where lost bits of nonsense and memories bide.
Old stamps wink and dance, like a mischievous sprite,
Saying, 'Take us, dear reader, on journeys tonight!'

So if you should wander where the old boxes dwell,
Don't be shy of the ruckus; it's fun, can't you tell?
Among these lost letters, a world you can shop,
And who knows? You might just find your old mop!

Chronicles of a Forgotten Voyage

There once was a ship, but not quite afloat,
With seagulls that giggled at its rusty old coat.
Its captain, a parrot, would squawk with delight,
Sailing through puddles in the middle of night.

The map was upside down, but that's how it goes,
For pirates and treasure had long lost their prose.
Instead of gold doubloons, they found a lost sock,
And a treasure of jellybeans shocked them with shock.

"To the land of misfits!" the captain did cheer,
With a crew made of plush toys who never showed fear.
They tumbled through dreams in their feathery hats,
Finding joy in the silly, like kings and their cats.

So if ever your journey seems adrift in a mist,
Just follow the laughter and don't be remiss.
You might just encounter a joyous parade,
Of echoes and giggles that never quite fade!

Relics of Yesterday's Dreams

In a closet of wonders, dreams lay on the floor,
A bicycle squeaks, though it hasn't been four.
A teddy bear grumbles about years gone by,
Claiming it's tired of that same old goodbye.

Old roller skates whisper, 'Let's go for a ride!'
While a skateboard argues, 'Come, join me!' with pride.
Underneath a bed, an old monster snores,
Dreaming of candy, and opening doors.

There's a pinball machine that still plays 'dings' loud,
While an umbrella spins tales of storms and proud.
Each relic has laughter tucked deep in its seams,
Waiting for children to wake up those dreams.

So gather your relics, don't hide them away,
For each silly memory deserves its display.
Embrace all the ruckus, and let laughter start,
For yesterday's dreams are a treasure in heart!

The Hushed Stories of a Suitcase

In a corner it sits, a suitcase so grey,
With stickers and stamps, oh the places it'd sway!
It grumbled of journeys to beaches and peaks,
And shared tales of mishaps like lost socks and leaks.

'Oh, remember the time when we missed that last flight?'

It chuckled while dreaming of that fateful night.
There's a tag from a city that's always been rainy,
'Two umbrellas needed!' it laughs, feeling zany.

Once a young traveler lost change in its folds,
A fortune in laughter, a story retold.
The socks still giggle, they're tucked in its side,
Racing to see who will fit in, unsure of their pride.

So sneak in a story, a secret to share,
With a suitcase so merry, it's quite a rare pair.
For the best of adventures need not be grand,
Just a suitcase of laughter and dreams on demand!

The Silent Chronicles of Home

In corners where shadows play,
Lies a box from yesterday.
It whispers secrets without a sound,
Of socks and toys that once were found.

A rubber duck with a wobbly grin,
Recites its tales of swimming in.
A plastic fork, quite worn and sad,
Yearns for the feasts it once had.

A dusty shoe, with a tragic loss,
Waits for the foot that once made it boss.
It chuckles softly, not quite forlorn,
Imagining paths it might have worn.

Home's shadows dance with a silly flair,
As long-lost items begin to share.
In silence they giggle, each secret told,
Of days gone by and treasures of old.

Dusty Corners and Hidden Tales

In the corner, a broom leans shy,
Dreams of sweeping the clouds from the sky.
A paperclip hums soft and low,
Of letters sent long ago.

A forgotten vase, with dust like a crown,
Hopes for a flower to never come down.
It sighs for the days of vibrant display,
When it held sunny blooms, bright and gay.

Behind a couch, lost toys convene,
Plotting adventures both crazy and keen.
They hold a council, not one a bore,
Ready to spring forth to explore.

Dust motes twirl in the stale, warm air,
As laughter floats out from the neglected lair.
Hidden treasures, with tales to unveil,
In dusty nooks where memories sail.

Token of Lost Adventures

A crumpled map, with paths untold,
Points to journeys that once were bold.
With edges frayed and colors faded,
It grins at the wonders it once paraded.

A treasure chest of mismatched socks,
Hiding stories of lost good luck rocks.
They plot a heist for a clown's red nose,
Laughing as they embark on their pose.

A lonely globe spins without care,
Reciting countries that aren't quite there.
With vibrant colors that make you sigh,
It dreams of the journeys it can't comply.

With giggles and whispers, they reminisce,
About adventures that ended in bliss.
A token of laughter in life's grand ballet,
As they scheme and plot through the bright day.

The Misadventures of Forgotten Luggage

Scratched and battered, a suitcase sighs,
Chasing dreams under faraway skies.
It once had flair, with stickers galore,
Now it waits like it's lost in folklore.

A pair of flip-flops, mismatched and worn,
Talk about trips that left them torn.
They recall a beach with waves that roared,
Now they're just tales in a dusty hoard.

A comb that dreams of being a wand,
In wild hairstyles, it used to be fond.
Now it mocks the mundane days,
While plotting escapades in funny ways.

The luggage chuckles, all things aside,
Waiting for journeys to take it for a ride.
With tales of mishaps, it beams with pride,
The misadventures of a life tried.

Saplings of Lost Narratives

In a grove where whispers play,
Silly secrets dance all day,
Leaves fall down, with laughter spun,
Tales of mischief, just begun.

Roots entwined in stories stout,
Beneath the bark, giggles shout,
Squirrels throw acorns with glee,
Nature's jesters, wild and free.

The Forgotten Hollow's Wisdom

In a hollow, wise old trees,
Share their thoughts with graceful ease,
"Did you hear?" one whispers low,
"About the squirrel's acorn show?"

Branches creak with hidden laughs,
Echoes of their silly gaffs,
"Mice wear hats, all the rage!"
Nature's jesters on this stage.

Nostalgia's Knotted Veins

In the bark, a laugh appears,
Twisted knots from many years,
Stories woven in the grain,
Laughter stored in every vein.

Old leaves chuckle, ruffled hair,
"Remember when?" fills the air,
Forest friends with tails to tell,
Whimsy woven, cast a spell.

Fragments of an Enchanted Legacy

Old trunks hold a world so bright,
Cracking jokes in morning light,
Mossy antics, wild and spry,
"Why did the crow fly high?"

Nearby, the toad sings its tune,
"Life's a circus, join the swoon!"
Branches wave with wild delight,
Tales of laughter take to flight.

In the Shadow of Yesterdays

Beneath the old oak, there lies a box,
Filled with old socks and some mismatched rocks.
Each piece a story, a chuckle, a sigh,
A rubber duck quacks as the memories fly.

A hat that was worn by a cat on a dare,
With glittery feathers and a dash of flair.
Who knew that old trunk could hold such a spree?
A dance with a pickle? Oh, yes, it was free!

The shoes twirled around with a ghost of a jig,
While the socks held a party that was quite big.
We burst out in laughter, the past felt so near,
In shadows of yesterdays, we lost all our fear.

Each treasure we found sparked a laugh and a grin,
As we talked of adventures, let the fun begin!
For life is a mix of the silly and grand,
In the shadows of yesterdays, joy hand in hand.

Sagas From a Splintered Past.

Oh, the tales that a cabinet could tell,
Of pirates and plunder, all ringing a bell.
A broomstick as a ship sailed the seas of my room,
With a spatula crew, they all danced to the doom.

A photo of Uncle with bright purple hair,
In a tutu, no less, what a sight beyond compare!
The tales here are wild, a true circus of lore,
Each splintered relic leaves us wanting more.

A teacup that glows with a wink and a wave,
Speaks of grand feasts held in the heart of a cave.
With laughter and echoes of fun in the air,
We cherish these sagas that none could prepare.

So gather 'round, friends, let the laughter commence,
As we dive into stories, they make perfect sense.
In the splinters of time, let joy have its say,
For the past is a treasure, the fun on display!

Whispers from the Old Chest

What secrets do linger in that dusty old chest?
With odd bits and bobs, it feels like a quest.
A pair of old glasses with no lenses inside,
But a view to the past where our giggles abide.

A jester's hat flops over a shoe made of cheese,
Just a prank from a brother that brings me to my knees.
In whispers of laughter, the memories tune,
As the chest tells the tales beneath light of the moon.

A magic wand too, made of popsicle sticks,
Turns pumpkins to coaches and younger folks to tricks.
With every small treasure, our laughter expands,
In whispers from the chest, humor takes its stand.

So let us dive deeper, let the fun overflow,
As the past dances with us in its lively glow.
These whispers enchant us, like kids we shall be,
Unlocking the joy in sweet memory's spree!

Secrets Beneath the Lid

A box filled with oddities lies there with pride,
A stuffed cat wearing glasses that once was a guide.
It winks at the fish, who swims round and round,
In secrets beneath the lid, joy knows no bound.

There's a spoon that once stirred up a magical brew,
And a map to the land where humor is true.
With giggles as treasures, we sift through our past,
In the depths of this trunk, the laughter holds fast.

The shoe of a giant, it could stomp to the beat,
While a tiny doll tap dances with sticky feet.
Together they prance in a whimsical play,
In secrets beneath the lid, we wander away.

So let's lift that cover, let's cherish and share,
The hilarity hidden, a joy beyond compare.
With every odd treasure, a story we weave,
In secrets beneath the lid, let's forever believe!

A Journey in Fragments

Inside an old box, strange things reside,
A sock with a hole and a matchstick slide.
A rubber chicken and a half-eaten pie,
Whispers of laughter, oh my, oh my!

The stories they tell, with each little peek,
Of adventures absurd, and days of the week.
A wobbly old hat from a clown so spry,
A puff of confetti and then a goodbye!

A riddle or ruckus can start with one key,
A button that leads to a vivid spree.
With each clatter and clang, the fun starts to grow,
In this treasure chest, there's always a show!

So dive in the chaos, let giggles ignite,
For these quirky finds bring pure delight.
You'll chuckle and grin, on this wild escapade,
In a world full of nonsense, all worries do fade.

The Box of Fleeting Shadows

A box of shadows, giggles afloat,
With each little creak of the squeaky boat.
A light bulb whispers, 'Here comes the fun!'
While shadows dance 'round, bright in the sun.

Out pops a raccoon, in a tutu so grand,
With juggling bananas, he takes a stand.
The shadows all cackle as they spin and twirl,
In this wacky world, let imaginations unfurl!

Catch a glimpse of the mayhem, a cat in a tie,
Doing the cha-cha, oh me, oh my!
The fun never ends, it just comes and goes,
In the box of laughter, it's all just a pose!

So if you seek joy, just peek inside,
Where shadows are friendly, and laughter is wide.
Take this rare journey—bring friends near too,
In this box of fleeting, delightful déjà vu.

Whispers between the Pages

Between the pages, secrets reside,
With quirky characters that dance and slide.
An octopus wearing a cowboy hat,
Tells tales of mischief, oh, imagine that!

Each paragraph giggles, with humor so sly,
A two-headed dragon takes flight in the sky.
With whispers of wisdom, they jest and tease,
While pages in flip-flops stroll with ease!

A donut-shaped spaceship zooms through the air,
Where marshmallow planets invite you to dare.
Every sentence a treasure—each giggle a gem,
It's a wild ride where dreams go stem to stem!

So grab a good book and let laughter unfold,
In the whispers between, a joy to behold.
Where stories come alive, in a big, funny way,
And mischief awaits in the words that play.

Daydreams in a Closed Vessel

In a closed vessel, dreams take flight,
A rubber duck pondering day and night.
It quacks up a storm, and bubbles appear,
While magic and mischief swim near and dear!

A jellybean pirate on a chocolate spree,
Hopes to find treasure beneath the gum tree.
With giggles of glee, each daydream does spark,
In this fanciful vessel, there's always a lark!

The walls are alive with boisterous tunes,
As fish in top hats perform silly swoons.
Cucumbers waltz in a gala of light,
A spectacle strange in this vessel so tight!

So let your mind wander, unlock every seam,
In this closed-up realm of whimsical dream.
With laughter as wind, let your spirit set free,
In the daydreams that dance, just you, them, and me!

Chronicles of the Old Chest

In the attic up high, a chest sits,
With treasures inside, some old, some bits.
A rubber chicken, a hat with a flair,
And a photo of grandma with purple hair.

I opened it wide, what a funny sight,
A sock with a hole, oh what a delight!
Old toys that have stories, they giggle and grin,
Inviting me back to the chaos within.

Nostalgia in a Dusty Box

A dusty old box under my bed,
Holds all of the things that my childhood bred.
A squeaky toy dinosaur, crayon debris,
And a diary filled with crushes on Lee.

I found a fake mustache, a joke from my friend,
With a note that said, "Wear this 'til the end!"
Laughter erupts from forgotten old pranks,
As I sift through the past with amused, happy thanks.

Clay and Echoes from the Past

A lump of old clay on the top of a shelf,
Sculpted by fingers of a younger self.
A wobbly duck with a grin oh so wide,
Reminds me of laughter I couldn't always hide.

Echoes of children, their giggles still gleam,
In shapes made from dreams, they wiggle and beam.
With each little piece, a story unfurls,
Of clay-covered days, and mud-smeared swirls.

Secrets Stowed Away

In a box full of secrets, beneath the old stairs,
Are rubber bands, buttons, and half-baked affairs.
A broken toy robot, with one metal leg,
And a jar full of marbles, the rainbow's egg.

What mysteries hide in this cluttered old space?
Perhaps socks with lost mates or a bright smiling face.
In the corners of chaos, where laughter resides,
Are stories of childhood that time gently hides.

The Keeper's Silent Chronicle

In a dusty corner, a trunk so bright,
Holds secrets hidden, a curious sight.
A sock with a tale, a shoe with a song,
Each item inside seems to feel like a throng.

A hat that can dance, with a jig of its own,
And mismatched mittens, quite well-known.
A rubber chicken whispers some jokes,
While old postcards chuckle, filled with pokes.

A magnifying glass, once so grand,
Zooms in on history, a funny brand.
Potato peels share a rumor or two,
Of a prankster who slipped on gooey stew.

In this keeper's chest, laughter does bloom,
Where memories twirl, making joy resume.
So if you should stumble upon this delight,
Prepare for a giggle that lasts through the night.

Traces of the Past Unveiled

A quilt from Grandma, with odd patches and seams,
Hides stories of laughter, and not-so-funny themes.
A button-eyed monster, sewn with great care,
Is plotting its revenge from a knotted stare.

Old letters crumpled, with ink smudged and worn,
Speak of a couple who once tried to adorn.
A rogue pasta noodle that never stood straight,
Claims it was a fashion of culinary fate.

Pictures of parties where socks became ties,
Captured the moments that brought forth the sighs.
The lid creaks open, releasing the cheer,
As dust bunnies laugh at the ghosts that appear.

In this treasure chest filled with humor and glee,
Lies a past that's both silly and wild as the sea.
So come join the fun, with a wink in your eye,
And dance with the relics, let laughter fly high.

Memory's Wooden Casket

A wooden chest sits, with a mischievous grin,
Inside are the wonders, where laughter begins.
A small rubber duck, wearing a crown,
Demanding a royal bath with a frown.

An ancient alarm clock that chirps out of time,
Announces it's lunchtime with a comedic rhyme.
Old crayons leap out, in colors so bright,
Sketching wild dreams in the soft morning light.

A pair of old dice, with numbers misplaced,
Claim every roll is a new game to taste.
Socks without partners gossip away,
Mocking the slippers that refuse to stay.

This casket of giggles, with treasures untold,
Holds memories wrapped in a blanket of gold.
So lift up the lid, let the laughter unfurl,
And join in the fun, let your heart spin and twirl.

Chronicles of the Buried Heart

Beneath the old cedar, a chest lies in wait,
Filled with odd trinkets and stories of fate.
A spoon with a caper, a cup with a crack,
Whispering secrets of laughter to track.

Lines of a comic, once tickled the town,
Drawn by a kid who wore a bright frown.
Silly old masks, with expressions so grand,
Are plotting a giggle, a playful band.

A sock puppet stirs, with a wink of its eye,
Reciting a tale of the pie in the sky.
Rumor has it, a sweater's a prince,
Who knitted some magic, it couldn't convince.

Each item a chapter, a laugh to behold,
Where memories mingle and joy is retold.
So sift through the treasure, let humor ignite,
In this buried heart, there's pure delight.

The Enigma of the Great Oak

Beneath the branches wide and grand,
Squirrels plot with acorns in hand.
They launch their raids, oh what a scene,
As nuts go flying, it's quite the routine.

A raccoon in a hat sips tea with glee,
While a rabbit debates who'll win the spree.
The tree just chuckles, a wise old soul,
Amused by each critter chasing their goal.

A woodpecker's beat, quite the odd tune,
Makes the owls grin while they swoon.
The winds carry laughter on a playful dart,
While pinecones drop like confetti, a party to start.

Leaves of Yesterday's Lore

In autumn's dance, the leaves do spin,
With tales of the past tucked deep within.
They whisper secrets to the playful breeze,
Where giggles rise above the trembling tease.

A caterpillar dressed in a bow,
Tries to charm the ladybugs, quite the show.
But with each twist, and tumble, they fall,
And roll down the path, laughter for all.

The stories they share of days long gone,
Are filled with blunders from dusk till dawn.
A wise old leaf, with a twinkle in sight,
Calls all to join in, a whimsical night.

Shadows of a Weathered Voyage

A parrot tells tales of a ship so grand,
Sailing through troubles, with a light-hearted band.
A crab in a sailor's hat takes the lead,
With a swagger so bold, and quite the speed.

The waves of laughter rock the old bark,
As fish come to listen, a splash in the dark.
The moon chuckles softly, the stars hold their breath,
As stories unfold from the shore to the depth.

With each hearty wave, a new joke is spun,
A sea of chuckles, so full of fun.
But as morning comes, the shadows retreat,
Leaving echoes of giggles, a joyous heartbeat.

Whimsy between the Branches

In the crook of a branch where the shadows play,
A gnome and a fox mix mischief each day.
With a hat that's too big and shoes that squeak,
They share tales of treasure that no one can seek.

A raccoon serves snacks on a leaf-made dish,
While a tiny bird sings, fulfilling a wish.
Their giggles erupt like the sun's bright rays,
Filling the forest with whimsical plays.

A dance for the critters, a jig in the glade,
Where laughter rings out, and worries do fade.
From morning till twilight, they spin and they twirl,
Creating pure joy at the end of each swirl.

Layers of Time in a Sturdy Case

In a box by the door, old socks reside,
Waiting for the day, when they'll take a ride.
With candy wrappers clinging, and spoons of gold,
They whisper of journeys, both bold and old.

Forgotten ties hide secrets, slick and neat,
With a cactus plant nestled, too frail on its feet.
The tales of a cat who once wore a hat,
And danced on the windowsill, imagine that!

Each layer reveals laughter, a jumbled song,
A glove with a hole, where fingers belong.
They giggle at wrinkles, at stains and cheer,
Sturdy wood keeps the madness all near.

Time tickles the edges, a playful parade,
As shadows and memories brilliantly fade.
With every new shuffle and every new chase,
Life finds its rhythm, inside this case.

Echoes of Lifetimes Past

In the corner, a shoe with a story to tell,
Of dances and prances, oh so very well.
While a button from jackets, with tales of the bold,
Nestles in the silence, growing old.

A compass goes spinning, with no sense of place,
Lost on adventures, a bewildered face.
Stickers of sunsets and joyous goodbyes,
Flake off the surface, revealing the lies.

Each echo of laughter from far, distant years,
Dances with shadows, and sometimes with tears.
The objects, they bicker, in playful debate,
Of love, loss, and socks that unfortunately mate.

Through curtain of dust, memories float high,
A sandwich left lonely, with crumbs made to cry.
With each little rummage, a giggle breaks free,
In echoes of lifetimes, we're always with glee.

Tales Leafed Through Dust

A book, oh so tattered, holds stories galore,
Of bananas in pajamas, and pies made of lore.
It flutters its pages, like wings in a breeze,
Tickling the air, with secrets to tease.

Underneath a bright lamp, an old teapot sits,
Dreaming of parties, its porcelain bits.
The sugar cubes crumble, like whispers from past,
As laughter from children seems forever to last.

Crumpled receipts that scribble a score,
Of meals that were shared, and sometimes much more.
Lost socks take the stage, in a tap dancing show,
Tales leafed through dust, as they put on a glow.

With every new turn of a forgettable page,
Life plays the piano, like a whimsical stage.
All stories combined, in a cluttered old space,
Share a cozy old warmth, with a giggling grace.

Hidden Voices of Worn Carriers

In a bag full of marbles, lost and unclaimed,
Whispers of players, once wildly famed.
The nylon still crackles with memories bright,
As it dreams of the games, in midday light.

Shoelaces tangled like gossiping friends,
Share tales of tripping, and how it all ends.
Underneath the sofa, a lonely old bear,
Listens to the laughter that floats through the air.

A dropped sandwich crust holds a secret so bold,
Of picnics gone wild, in the sunshine, uncontrolled.
In the pockets of jackets, past treasures reside,
Where glitter and giggles previously bide.

The carriers whisper of journeys they've seen,
Of snacks and adventures, and moments serene.
With each hidden voice, a story takes flight,
In a world full of laughter, oh what a delight!

Secrets of the Worn-Out Suitcase

A suitcase sat with a tear in its seam,
Filled with odd trinkets and things that may seem,
A rubber chicken, and socks with bright stripes,
Each item waiting for a story to swipe.

The zippers complain, in a comical tone,
As if to say, "Leave my secrets alone!"
With every tug, laughter jumps through the air,
What joy can be found in this dusty old square!

Old ticket stubs sing songs of those trips,
Where soup spilled over and laughter just drips.
Remember the time it got lost at the fair?
It danced on the carousel, spinning in air!

So here's to that suitcase, well-traveled and wise,
Full of weird wonders and whimsical ties,
Let's take a peek, and giggle a bit,
For in every wrinkle, there's humor to fit!

Lifetimes Between Clasped Lids

Oh, what a ruckus behind those sleek locks,
A treasure chest filled with old yellowed socks!
Each lid that you open reveals quite the sight,
Like a comedy show in the soft evening light.

There's a hula hoop with a story to spin,
And half-eaten snacks that were left to grow thin.
A note from a pen pal that once went astray,
Claiming she danced with a frog in the fray!

Old travel guides missing half of their pages,
Haunted by memories of wild, funny stages.
"Let's go to Paris!" the map tries to shout,
But tragedy struck, and the shot was a drought!

With laughter and chuckles, we pry it all free,
The things that we find bring back joy and glee.
So let's stash new stories for future delight,
In this chest of wonders, let's revel tonight!

Stories Beneath Layered Dust

Under the layers, a tale starts to bloom,
A dragonfly's wing in the corner of gloom.
It whispered a secret of flying too high,
And how it once tried to dance with the sky.

A spoon with a tale of a spaghetti fight,
Its handle still glistens with sauce of delight.
Ah! The fights and the feasts, all baked in the past,
Each item a memory, made to hold fast.

An old magician's hat with a rabbit inside,
Did he vanish or fly? It's hard to decide!
With every new stumble, there's laughter around,
As secrets unfold from where they were bound.

So dust off the corners, don't let stories sleep,
For in this old box, laughter's treasures do leap.
Let's giggle together at everything found,
For each quirky artifact must wear a crown!

Fragments of Time in a Chest

In a chest of odd fragments, time seems to play,
A tooth from a dragon that chewed on the day.
With echoes of giggles and bits of delight,
It weaves a strange web in the softening light.

Old board games where laughter once spilled on the floor,
A Monopoly piece searching for more!
Each dice is a dream that might take to the skies,
With every roll, there's a new tale to rise.

Oh, the wacky adventures of socks gone astray,
In search of their partners, they frolicked to play,
A mystery hidden in cotton and hue,
What tales they could tell if only they knew!

So here's to the fragments, each one holds its cheer,
Let's gather them all, pull them close and draw near.
For laughter is timeless in every fine quest,
In this chest of fragments, let's have the best fest!

Stories Carried by the Wind

In a town where whispers roam,
Laughed a breeze that felt like home.
It carried tales from near and far,
A shoe, a hat, a stolen car.

Underneath the banyan tree,
A squirrel claimed a pirate's spree.
With acorns spun as golden crowns,
He ruled the world of silly towns.

The old man chuckled at the song,
As passed the breeze, all day long.
With every flap and fluttery cheer,
He swore he heard a squirrel sneer!

So when you hear a giggle's sound,
Just know that joy is all around.
In every gust a story stirs,
A tale of laughter, furry furs.

The Silent Witness of Travels

Down the road where travelers roam,
A suitcase sighed, far from its home.
It held the secrets, laughter and shouts,
Of all the trips, with twists and doubts.

With stickers clinging, peeling now,
It dreamed of mountains, rivers, how?
Of sunburned days and rainy strife,
The silent witness of a funny life.

In Paris, it had danced with wine,
In Cairo, it met an ancient line.
Yet here it sat, forlorn and still,
Missing its tales, chasing a thrill.

If bags could talk, oh what they'd say,
Of clumsy moments gone astray.
So pack your dreams and travel light,
For every journey brings delight!

Lost and Found Again

A sock embarked on a grand quest,
To find its mate and give it rest.
It wandered through the washing maze,
And laughed at all the silly ways.

It met a spoon who thought it fly,
And said, "Come join the silver sky!"
Together they made quite the pair,
Chasing ghosts without a care.

In the dryer, they found old games,
With twirls and flips, they played like flames.
Yet hopes grew bleak, socks turned to pairs,
As laundry day revealed the snares.

At last, the sock found its true friend,
A dance of joy that would not end.
Lost? Found! It's all in the spin,
An adventure where laughs begin.

Chronicles of a Hidden Life

In a drawer where no one looks,
Lies a trove of funny books.
With scribbles, doodles, jokes galore,
Their wisdom whispered behind a door.

A pizza slice with extra cheese,
Once tried to bargain with the breeze.
It claimed to fly, to soar like birds,
But ended up wrapped in silly words.

A lonely sock, a taco too,
Did silly dances, oh, what a crew!
They spun around 'til morning light,
Creating chaos, pure delight.

So peek inside that unknown space,
And join the fun, the silly race.
For in those tales of hidden strife,
Lies the laughter of a hidden life.

www.ingramcontent.com/pod-product-compliance
Lightning Source LLC
Chambersburg PA
CBHW051634160426
43209CB00004B/642